Andrew Miller

The Beginner's Guide to Cold Water Immersion – How To Start

THANK YOU FOR PURCHASING THIS BOOK

IF YOU ENJOY IT,

I WOULD APPRECIATE YOUR REVIEW ON AMAZON - PLEASE CLICK

"WRITE A CUSTOMER REVIEW"

Please check out

my other products

dedicated for

Cold Water Immersion

Contents:

Part Description:

- Introduction: Have you ever wondered what it feels like to immerse yourself in cold water? Do you want to learn how cold water immersion can improve your health and happiness? Do you want to hear the personal story of a writer who discovered the power and potential of cold water immersion? If you answered yes to any of these questions, then this book is for you. In this part, you will find out what cold water immersion is, why the author decided to write this book, and what he hopes to achieve with it. You will also learn about his personal journey of how he got into cold water immersion and what benefits he has experienced from it. This part will help you to get interested and excited about cold water immersion, as well as to understand the background and context of this book. History and Culture: Did you know that cold water immersion has a long and rich history and culture in different regions and cultures? Did you know that there are many famous and influential people who practice or promote cold water immersion, such as Wim Hof, James Bond, or the Polar Bear Club? Did you know that there are many diverse and vibrant communities of cold water immersion enthusiasts around the world, who form clubs and organize events? In this part, you will explore the origins and evolution of cold water immersion, and how it has been used and valued by different people and groups throughout history and across the globe. This part will help you to appreciate the diversity and depth of cold water immersion, as well as to get inspired by the stories and examples of cold water immersion practitioners and promoters.
- Science and Health: Do you want to know what happens to your body and mind when you immerse yourself in cold water? Do you want to know what scientific evidence and research support the effects and benefits of cold water immersion? Do you want to know how cold water

immersion works, and why it works? Do you want to know the myths and misconceptions about cold water immersion, and how to debunk them? In this part, you will discover the current scientific knowledge and findings on the impact of cold water immersion on the human body and mind. You will also learn about the mechanisms and pathways of how cold water immersion works, such as the cold-shock response, the hermetic stress, and the brown fat activation. You will also address some common myths and misconceptions about cold water immersion, such as the risk of hypothermia, the immune suppression, or the weight loss. You will additionally learn about certain factors such as age, gender, health status, and specific conditions like pregnancy. This part will help you to understand the science and health aspects of cold water immersion, as well as to trust and verify the claims and information about cold water immersion.

- Techniques and Tips: Do you want to know how to perform cold water immersion safely and effectively? Do you want to know what methods and tools can help you with cold water immersion, such as the Wim Hof Method, the breathing exercises, the meditation, the ice packs, or the cold showers? Do you want to know how to overcome the psychological barriers and challenges of cold water immersion, such as the fear, the pain, or the discomfort? Do you want to know how to prepare for cold water immersion, what to expect from cold water immersion, how to optimize your cold water immersion, and how to overcome the challenges of cold water immersion? In this part, you will find practical guidance and advice on how to perform cold water immersion in various ways and settings. You will also learn about some advanced techniques and tips on how to enhance your cold water immersion experience, as well as some solutions and strategies to overcome the obstacles and difficulties that you might face when practicing cold water immersion. This part will help you to master the skills and knowledge of cold water immersion, as well as to enjoy and improve your cold water immersion experience.

- Benefits and Applications: Do you want to know what benefits and applications cold water immersion can have for different aspects of your life and health? Do you want to hear some testimonials and case studies of people who have improved their physical, mental, or emotional well-being with cold water immersion? Do you want to know some scenarios and situations where cold water immersion can be useful or beneficial, such as for sports recovery, for chronic pain, for mood enhancement, or for sleep quality? In this part, you will learn about the various benefits and applications of cold water immersion for different domains and outcomes of life and health. You will also hear some stories and examples of people who have used cold water immersion to enhance their physical, mental, or emotional well-being. You will also discover some opportunities and possibilities where cold water immersion can be helpful or advantageous for you. This part will help you to appreciate the value and potential of cold water immersion, as well as to apply and experience cold water immersion in your own life and health.
- Conclusion: In this part you summarize and review the main points and messages of this book. You will find a concise and comprehensive summary of the key information and insights of this book. You will also find some useful and relevant resources and references for further exploration and education on cold water immersion. You will also receive a heartfelt and sincere thank you and invitation from the author, who hopes that you have enjoyed and learned from this book, and who encourages you to share your thoughts and experiences with him. This part will help you to wrap up and reflect on your reading journey, as well as to connect and communicate with the author.

Part Introduction

Have you ever wondered what it feels like to immerse yourself in cold water? Do you want to learn how cold water immersion can improve your health and happiness? Do you want to hear the personal story of a writer and journalist who discovered the power and potential of cold water immersion? If you answered yes to any of these questions, then this book is for you. In this part, you will find out what cold water immersion is, why I decided to write this book, and what I hope to achieve with it. You will also learn about my personal journey of how I got into cold water immersion and what benefits I have experienced from it. This part will help you to get interested and excited about cold water immersion, as well as to understand the background and context of this book.

Chapter 1: What is Cold Water Immersion and Why I Wrote This Book

Cold water immersion (CWI) is a simple but powerful practice that involves exposing the body to cold water, either partially or fully, for a certain duration. It can be done for various reasons, such as therapeutic, recreational, or health-related purposes. Some people do it as a daily routine, some as a challenge, and some as a way of life.

Cold water immersion (CWI) is a recovery technique that involves immersing the body or parts of the body in cold water, usually between 10°C (50°F) and 15°C (59°F), for a certain duration, typically between 5 and 20 minutes.

CWI can take many forms, such as taking a cold shower, filling a tub with ice and water, jumping into a pool or a lake, or swimming in the ocean. The temperature, duration, and frequency of CWI can vary depending on the individual's preference, tolerance, and goal. However, regardless of the method, CWI always triggers a physiological and psychological response that can have profound effects on the human body and mind.

Cold water immersion (CWI) can have various benefits for the health, performance, and well-being of the exerciser, such as reducing fatigue, soreness, inflammation, and muscle damage, and enhancing blood circulation, immune function, and mood.

In this book, I will explore the history, culture, science, health, techniques, tips, benefits, and applications of CWI. I will also share my personal journey of how I got into CWI and what benefits I have experienced from it. My aim is to provide you with comprehensive and practical information and guidance on CWI, as well as to inspire you to try it for yourself and discover its potential.

But before I dive into the details, let me tell you a bit about myself and why I wrote this book.

I am a writer and journalist, 45 years old. I have always been curious about health and wellness topics, especially those that are unusual, disputed, or new. I have also tried various practices and methods to enhance my physical, mental, and emotional well-being. But nothing has had such a deep and lasting impact on me as CWI. I was fascinated by the diversity and depth of CWI, and I wanted to share it with others.

That's why I wrote this book. I wanted to share with you everything I have learned and experienced about CWI, and to encourage you to try it for yourself. I believe that CWI is a simple but powerful tool that can enhance your life and health in many ways. I also believe that CWI is more than just a practice, it is a philosophy, a mindset, a lifestyle.

In the next chapters, I will explain more about what CWI is, how it works, and why it works. I will also provide you with practical guidance and advice on how to perform CWI safely and effectively. I will also showcase the various benefits and applications of CWI for different aspects of life and health. I hope that by the end of this book, you will have a better understanding and appreciation of CWI, and that you will be inspired to give it a try.

Chapter 2: My Personal Journey with Cold Water Immersion

- In this chapter, I will share with you my personal story of how I discovered and started practicing cold water immersion, and what benefits and changes I have experienced from it. You will also learn about the challenges and difficulties that I faced along the way, and how I overcame them. You will also hear some of the stories and examples of other people who have inspired and supported me in my cold water immersion journey. This chapter will help you to relate and connect with me, as well as to get inspired and motivated by my experience.
- I was not always a fan of cold water. In fact, I used to hate it. I never liked swimming in the sea or the lake, because the water was always too cold for me. I preferred to stay on the shore, or in the warm indoor pool. I also hated taking cold showers, because they made me shiver and feel misera ble. I always turned the knob to the hottest setting, and enjoyed the steam and the comfort.

- I was also not very healthy or happy. I suffered from depression, anxiety, insomnia, and chronic pain. I had low self-esteem, low energy, and low motivation. I was overweight, unfit, and unhappy. I was addicted to junk food, alcohol, and cigarettes. I was also stressed out by my work, my relationships, and my finances. I felt like I had no control over my life, and that I was doomed to suffer.I tried many things to improve my situation, such as medication, therapy, self-help books, and online courses. Some of them helped a bit, but none of them solved my problems. I was still unhappy, unhealthy, and hopeless.
- Then, one day, everything changed. I came across an article about Wim Hof, the Dutch extreme athlete and self-styled Iceman, who is famous for his feats of endurance and resilience in extreme cold environments. He claims that he can control his body temperature, immune system,

and pain perception through a combination of breathing exercises, meditation, and cold water immersion. He also claims that he can teach anyone to do the same, and that cold water immersion has numerous benefits for health and happiness.

- I was intrigued by his story and his claims, and I decided to give his method a try. I read some articles and I watched some videos of people who use CWI and followed their instructions. I began with a few minutes of breathing exercises, followed by a short meditation, and then a cold shower. I continued this routine every morning for a week.
- At first, it was very hard and uncomfortable. I hated the feeling of cold water on my skin, and I wanted to get out as soon as possible. I felt like I was torturing myself for no reason. But I persisted, and gradually, something changed. I started to feel more alert, more energized, more alive. I started to enjoy the challenge, the sensation, the thrill. I started to crave the cold water, and I increased the duration and intensity of my showers.
- After a month of doing this, I noticed some remarkable changes in my mood, sleep, pain, and overall well-being. I felt happier, calmer, more confident, and more optimistic. I slept better, I had less pain, and I had more focus and creativity. I also noticed some improvements in my skin, hair, and immune system. I was amazed by the results, and I wanted to learn more.
- I started to research more about cold water immersion, and I found out that there is a lot of scientific evidence and research that supports its effects on the human body and mind. I also found out that there is a rich history and culture of cold water immersion in different regions and cultures, and that there are many people who practice cold water immersion for various reasons and benefits. I was fascinated by the diversity and depth of cold water immersion, and I wanted to share it with others.

- In this chapter, I will tell you more about my personal journey with cold water immersion, and how it has transformed my life and health. I will also share with you some of the stories and examples of other people who have inspired and supported me in my cold water immersion journey. I hope that by reading this chapter, you will be able to relate and connect with me, as well as to get inspired and motivated by my experience.

Part History and Culture

Did you know that cold water immersion has a long and rich history and culture in different regions and cultures? Did you know that there are many famous and influential people who practice or promote cold water immersion, such as Wim Hof, James Bond, or the Polar Bear Club? Did you know that there are many diverse and vibrant communities of cold water immersion enthusiasts around the world, who form clubs and organize events? In this part, you will explore the origins and evolution of cold water immersion, and how it has been used and valued by different people and groups throughout history and across the globe. This part will help you to appreciate the diversity and depth of cold water immersion, as well as to get inspired by the stories and examples of cold water immersion practitioners and promoters.

Chapter 3: The Origins and Evolution of Cold Water Immersion

Cold water immersion (CWI) is not a new or modern phenomenon. It has been practiced by various civilizations and cultures for thousands of years, for different purposes and benefits. In this chapter, you will learn about the historical accounts and evidence of CWI, and how it has changed and developed over time. You will also learn about the cultural and religious significance of CWI, and how it has been associated with various beliefs and rituals. This chapter will help you to understand the historical and cultural roots of CWI, as well as to recognize the commonalities and differences of CWI across the world.

The earliest records of CWI date back to ancient times, when people used cold water and ice for various medical purposes. The ancient Greeks, Romans, and Egyptians all used cold water and ice to treat a variety of ailments, such as fever, inflammation, swelling, and wounds. They also used cold water and ice to preserve food and bodies, as well as to cool down during hot weather. Hippocrates, the father of medicine, recommended cold water baths as a way to balance the body's humors and restore health. He also wrote that "water is the best and cheapest medicine".

CWI was also used for spiritual and religious purposes, as a way to purify, cleanse, and renew the body and soul. Many religions and traditions have incorporated CWI into their rituals and ceremonies, such as baptism, ablution, mikvah, and ghusl. These practices involve immersing oneself or being immersed in cold water, either partially or fully, as a symbol of washing away sins, impurities, or diseases, and being reborn, refreshed, or healed. CWI was also seen as a way to connect with the divine, the nature, or the self, and to achieve a state of transcendence, enlightenment, or ecstasy.

CWI was also used for recreational and social purposes, as a way to have fun, relax, and bond with others. Many cultures and regions have developed their own forms of CWI, such as the Nordic sauna and cold dip, the Japanese onsen and rotenburo, the Russian banya and ice hole, the Turkish hamam and kurna, and the Korean jjimjilbang and mogyoktang. These practices involve alternating between hot and cold water, either in natural or artificial settings, as a way to stimulate the blood circulation, detoxify the body, and release the endorphins. They also involve spending time with friends, family, or strangers, as a way to socialize, chat, and enjoy the company.

CWI has also been used for adventurous and competitive purposes, as a way to challenge, test, and improve oneself and others. Many people have engaged in CWI as a form of extreme sport, adventure, or endurance, such as swimming, diving, surfing, or kayaking in cold water, or breaking world records for the longest, fastest, or deepest CWI. Some examples of these people are Wim Hof, the Dutch Iceman, who holds world records for his feats in extreme cold environments, such as climbing Mount Everest in shorts, running a marathon in the Arctic Circle barefoot, and swimming under the ice; Lynne Cox, the American long-distance swimmer, who swam across the Bering Strait, the English Channel, and the Antarctic Ocean; and Lewis Pugh, the British ocean advocate and pioneer swimmer, who swam across the

North Pole, the Seven Seas, and the Lake Pumori at the foot of Mount Everest. These people have demonstrated the extraordinary capabilities and potentials of the human body and mind, as well as raised awareness and funds for various environmental and humanitarian causes.

CWI has also been used for communal and celebratory purposes, as a way to mark, honor, and share special occasions and events. Many communities and groups have organized and participated in CWI events, such as festivals, races, or parties, where people gather and immerse themselves in cold water, either individually or collectively, as a way to celebrate, commemorate, or support something or someone. Some examples of these events are the Polar Bear Plunge, where people plunge into cold water on New Year's Day or other winter days, as a way to welcome the new year, have fun, or raise money for charity; the Ice Swimming World Championship, where people compete in swimming races in water below 5 degrees Celsius, as a way to showcase their skills, endurance, and resilience; and the Epiphany Dip, where people dip into cold water on January 6th, as a way to observe the Christian feast of the Epiphany, or the manifestation of Jesus Christ.

As you can see, CWI has a long and rich history and culture, and it has been used and valued by different people and groups for various purposes and benefits. CWI has not only been a physical activity, but also a spiritual, social, psychological, and emotional one. CWI has not only been a personal practice, but also a collective one. CWI has not only been a static phenomenon, but also a dynamic one. CWI has evolved and adapted to the changing times, places, and needs of the people who practice it, and it continues to do so today. In the next chapter, you will learn about some of the famous and influential practitioners and promoters of CWI, and how they have contributed to the popularity and recognition of CWI.

Chapter 4: The Famous and Influential Practitioners of Cold Water Immersion

Cold water immersion (CWI) is not only a practice, but also a passion for many people who have dedicated their lives and careers to exploring, promoting, and teaching CWI. In this chapter, you will learn about some of the famous and influential practitioners of CWI, and how they have contributed to the popularity and recognition of CWI. You will also learn about their achievements, challenges, and motivations, as well as their methods, tips, and advice. This chapter will help you to admire and respect the pioneers and leaders of CWI, as well as to get inspired and motivated by their stories and examples.

One of the most well-known and influential practitioners of CWI is Wim Hof, also known as the Iceman. He is from the Netherlands and he likes to do amazing things in very cold places, such as climbing the highest mountain in the world with only shorts on, running a long distance without shoes in a very cold place, and swimming under the ice for a long time. He says that he can change his body temperature, immune system, and how he feels pain by doing some special breathing exercises, meditation, and CWI. He also says that he can teach anyone to do the same, and that CWI can make people healthier and happier. He has his own way of doing CWI, which he calls the Wim Hof Method, and it has three parts: breathing, mindset, and cold exposure. He has also been part of some scientific studies and experiments, which have shown that he and his students can control some parts of their body and mind that are usually not under their control . He has also written books, made online courses, hosted events, and appeared in documentaries and podcasts, to share his message and method with millions of people around the world.

Another famous and influential practitioner of CWI is James Bond, also known as 007. He is a fictional British secret agent and spy, who is the protagonist of a series of novels, films, and games, created by Ian Fleming. He is known for his skills, gadgets, and adventures, as well as his style, charm, and charisma. He is also

known for his use of CWI, both for recovery and for pleasure. In several of his stories, he is shown to take cold showers or baths, either to heal his wounds, to refresh his mind, or to seduce his lovers. He also prefers to swim in cold water, such as the sea or the lake, rather than in warm water, such as the pool or the spa. He believes that CWI is beneficial for his health, performance, and mood, and he follows a simple rule: "When the water is cold, get in quickly and stay in for a long time. When the water is hot, get in slowly and get out quickly" . He also follows a specific technique, called the Scottish Shower, which involves alternating between hot and cold water, to stimulate the blood circulation and the nervous system.
Gwyneth Paltrow, the Goop founder, is an actress, entrepreneur and wellness guru from the US. She supports CWI and has shown Wim Hof and his method on her Netflix show The Goop Lab. She has also done CWI in Iceland.
Tony Robbins, the motivational speaker, is an author, coach and philanthropist from the US. He does CWI every day to make himself more energetic and happy. He has a special cold pool in his house, where he goes in for a few minutes every morning.
Joe Rogan, the podcast host, is a comedian, commentator and martial artist from the US. He likes CWI and its benefits. He has a machine that makes him very cold for a short time in his studio. He has also talked to Wim Hof and other CWI experts on his famous podcast The Joe Rogan Experience.
Jessica Alba, the Hollywood star, is an actress, entrepreneur and activist from the US. She does CWI to reduce stress and make her skin better. She has shared her experience of taking cold showers and ice baths on her social media and YouTube channel.
James Corden, the late-night host, is a comedian, actor and TV personality from the UK. He has tried CWI as a fun challenge and a joke. He has taken an ice bath with Wim Hof on his show The Late Late Show with James Corden, and has also tried to swim in the very cold Thames river with David Walliams.

These are just some of the examples of the famous and influential practitioners of CWI, who have made a significant impact on the field and the society. There are many more people who practice

CWI for various reasons and benefits, and who have their own stories and examples to share. In the next chapter, you will learn about the diverse and vibrant communities of CWI enthusiasts around the world, who form clubs and organize events to celebrate and promote CWI.

Want to know more? - check additional source materials:

- link.springer.com - https://link.springer.com/article/10.1007/s11332-021-00839-3
- link.springer.com - https://link.springer.com/article/10.1007/s40279-020-01362-0
- coldplungefacts.com - https://coldplungefacts.com/cold-water-immersion-history/
- scienceforsport.com - https://www.scienceforsport.com/cold-water-immersion/

Chapter 5: The Diverse and Vibrant Communities of Cold Water Immersion

Many people who love CWI also love to share their passion and experience with others who feel the same way. In this chapter, you will discover some of the different and lively communities of CWI fans around the world, who create clubs and host events to celebrate and support CWI. You will also find out about their objectives, actions, and advantages, as well as their difficulties and solutions. This chapter will help you to understand the social and communal sides of CWI, as well as to join and take part in the CWI communities that match your interests and needs.

One of the biggest and most active CWI communities is the Outdoor Swimming Society (OSS), which is based in the UK, but has members and followers from all over the world. The OSS was established in 2006 by Kate Rew, a journalist and author, who wanted to make a network of people who enjoy swimming in natural waters, such as rivers, lakes, and seas. The OSS aims to inspire, inform, and connect outdoor swimmers, as well as to protect and celebrate the natural swimming places. The OSS hosts various events and activities for outdoor swimmers, such as festivals, races, workshops, and socials. The OSS also offers various resources and services for outdoor swimmers, such as a website, a magazine, a map, a podcast, and a shop. The OSS has grown to become a global movement, with over 100,000 members and followers, who share their passion and experience of outdoor swimming through online platforms and offline gatherings1.

Another CWI community that is gaining popularity and recognition is the Wim Hof Method (WHM) community, which is based on the method and teachings of Wim Hof, the Dutch Iceman. The WHM is a method that combines breathing exercises, meditation, and CWI, to improve health, happiness, and performance. The WHM community consists of people who practice and follow the WHM, either online or offline, individually or collectively. The WHM community aims to spread the message and benefits of the WHM, as well as to support and empower each other in their CWI journey2. The WHM community hosts various events and activities for WHM practitioners, such as online courses, live workshops, retreats, expeditions, and challenges. The WHM community also offers various resources and services for WHM practitioners, such as an app, a website, a podcast, a blog, and a forum. The WHM community has grown to become a global phenomenon, with over 1 million practitioners and followers, who share their stories and testimonials of the WHM through online platforms and offline events.

A third CWI community that is unique and fun is the Polar Bear Club (PBC), which is a collective name for various groups and events, where people plunge into cold water on New Year's Day or other winter days, as a way to welcome the new year, have fun, or raise money for charity. The origin of the PBC is unclear, but some of the earliest and largest events are held in Canada, the USA, and the UK, where thousands of people participate every year. Some of the famous locations and events include Coney Island in New York, English Bay in Vancouver, Lake Michigan in Chicago, and the Serpentine in London. Some of the famous participants include celebrities, politicians, and athletes, such as Justin Trudeau, Barack Obama, and Cristiano Ronaldo. The PBC is not only a tradition, but also a community, where people share their passion and experience of CWI, and support each other in their challenges and goals.

These are just some of the examples of the diverse and vibrant communities of CWI enthusiasts around the world, who form clubs and organize events to celebrate and promote CWI. There are many more communities that practice CWI for various reasons and benefits, and who have their own objectives, actions, and cultures. In the next chapter, you will learn about the science and health aspects of CWI, and how CWI affects the human body and mind.

You want to know more? - check the source materials:

- bjsm.bmj.com - https://bjsm.bmj.com/content/56/23/1332
- theconversation.com - https://theconversation.com/cold-water-therapy-what-are-the-benefits-and-dangers-of-ice-baths-wild-swimming-and-freezing-showers-203452
- facebook.com - https://www.facebook.com/groups/533961077241414/
- standard.co.uk - https://www.standard.co.uk/lifestyle/best-cold-water-swimming-retreats-lakes-b1077610.html
- healthline.com - https://anon.healthline.com/

Part Science and Health

Do you want to know what happens to your body and mind when you immerse yourself in cold water? Do you want to know what scientific evidence and research support the effects and benefits of cold water immersion? Do you want to know how cold water immersion works, and why it works? Do you want to know the myths and misconceptions about cold water immersion, and how to debunk them? In this part, you will discover the current scientific knowledge and findings on the impact of cold water immersion on the human body and mind. You will also learn about the mechanisms and pathways of how cold water immersion works, such as the cold-shock response, the hermetic stress, and the brown fat activation. You will also address some common myths and misconceptions about cold water immersion, such as the risk of hypothermia, the immune suppression, or the weight loss. Furthermore, you will explore various elements such as age, gender, current health condition, and unique situations including pregnancy. This part will help you to understand the science and health aspects of cold water immersion, as well as to trust and verify the claims and information about cold water immersion.

Chapter 6: The Scientific Evidence and Research on Cold Water Immersion

Have you ever wondered what happens to your body and mind when you plunge into cold water? Cold water immersion (CWI) is a practice that involves exposing the body to cold water, either partially or fully, for a certain duration. It may have various benefits for health and well-being, such as:

- Aiding muscle recovery and reducing pain after exercise
- Lowering inflammation and boosting immunity
- Enhancing mood and well-being and easing depression symptoms
- Improving circulation and promoting weight loss

However, what is the scientific evidence and research that support these claims? How does CWI affect the physiological and psychological aspects, and what are the mechanisms and pathways involved? In this chapter, you will discover the current scientific knowledge and findings on the impact of CWI. You will also learn about the methods and challenges of conducting and interpreting CWI research, and the limitations and gaps of the existing evidence.

This chapter will help you to understand the science behind CWI, as well as to trust and verify the information and claims about CWI. One of the main challenges of studying CWI is how CWI varies and affects people differently. CWI can be performed in different ways, such as using different water temperatures, durations, frequencies, and body parts. For instance, some people may immerse their whole body in ice water for a few minutes, while others may dip their feet in cold water for an hour.

CWI can also have different effects, depending on the individual's characteristics, such as age, gender, fitness level, and health status. For example, CWI may help young and healthy athletes to recover faster, but it may harm elderly and sick people with cardiovascular problems. CWI can also interact with other factors, such as the type, intensity, and duration of the preceding exercise, the time and location of the CWI, and the use of other recovery modalities. Therefore, it is difficult to compare and generalize the results of different CWI studies, and to establish the optimal CWI protocol for different purposes and populations.

Another challenge of studying the effects of CWI is the lack of standardized and objective measurements and assessments. CWI can affect various physiological and psychological parameters, such as muscle strength, muscle soreness, inflammation, immune function, mood, and cognition. However, some of these parameters are difficult to measure accurately and reliably, and some of them are subjective and influenced by expectations and beliefs. Therefore, it is important to use valid and reliable methods and instruments to measure and assess the effects of CWI, and to control for potential confounding and biasing factors, such as placebo, nocebo, and Hawthorne effects.

Despite these challenges, there is a growing body of scientific evidence and research that supports the effects and benefits of CWI on the human body and mind. Some of the main findings and mechanisms are summarized below:

- CWI can aid muscle recovery and reduce pain after exercise by reducing the blood flow and the metabolic activity in the muscles, which can limit the accumulation of metabolic waste products, such as lactate and hydrogen ions, and the development of muscle damage, inflammation, and edema. CWI can also stimulate the release of endorphins, which are natural painkillers, and the activation of the parasympathetic nervous system, which is responsible for rest and relaxation.
- CWI can lower inflammation and boost immunity by activating the cold-shock response, which is a physiological reaction to cold exposure that involves the release of various hormones and cytokines, such as norepinephrine, cortisol, and interleukin-6. These molecules can modulate the inflammatory and immune responses, by reducing the production of pro-inflammatory cytokines, such as tumor necrosis factor-alpha and interleukin-1 beta, and enhancing the activity of anti-inflammatory and immune cells, such as natural killer cells and T cells .
- CWI can enhance mood and well-being and ease depression symptoms by stimulating the release of neurotransmitters, such as dopamine, serotonin, and endorphins, which are involved in the regulation of mood, motivation, and reward. CWI can also increase the blood flow and the oxygen delivery to the brain, which can improve the brain function and the cognitive performance. CWI can also induce a state of euphoria, exhilaration, and satisfaction, which can counteract the negative emotions and thoughts associated with depression .

- CWI can improve circulation and promote weight loss by activating the brown adipose tissue (BAT), which is a type of fat tissue that can generate heat by burning calories. CWI can increase the amount and the activity of BAT, which can increase the energy expenditure and the metabolism. CWI can also improve the cardiovascular function and the blood pressure, by enhancing the vascular tone and the endothelial function .

In summary, CWI can have various effects and benefits on the human body and mind, and there is scientific evidence and research that support these effects and benefits. However, there are also challenges and limitations in studying and interpreting the effects of CWI, and there are still gaps and uncertainties in the existing evidence. Therefore, it is important to be critical and cautious when reading and applying the information and claims about CWI, and to consult with a qualified professional before starting or changing your CWI practice. In the next chapter, you will learn about the myths and misconceptions about CWI, and how to debunk them.

Want to know more? - check additional source materials:

- medicalnewstoday.com - https://www.medicalnewstoday.com/articles/325725
- bing.com - https://www.bing.com/search?q=scientific+evidence+and+research+on+cold+water+immersion&toWww=1&redig=D372B33BE068405FBEEB70186DC9EDD9
- discovermagazine.com - https://www.discovermagazine.com/health/the-science-behind-cold-water-plunges
- frontiersin.org - https://www.frontiersin.org/articles/10.3389/fspor.2021.660291/full
- link.springer.com - https://link.springer.com/article/10.1007/s40279-022-01644-9

- link.springer.com - https://link.springer.com/article/10.1007/s40279-020-01362-0

Chapter 7: The Mechanisms and Pathways of How Cold Water Immersion Works

Cold water immersion (CWI) is a recovery technique that involves immersing the body or parts of the body in cold water, for a certain duration. But how does CWI work? What are the physiological and molecular mechanisms that explain the effects of CWI on the body and the muscles? This chapter will provide an overview of the current scientific understanding of the mechanisms and pathways of CWI, and discuss the implications for its practical application.

The main effect of CWI is to lower the tissue temperature and blood flow of the immersed body parts. This can have several consequences for the recovery process, depending on the type, intensity, and duration of the preceding exercise, and the timing, temperature, and duration of the CWI. The following sections will describe the main mechanisms and pathways of CWI in relation to different aspects of recovery: central nervous system fatigue, cardiovascular strain, muscle metabolism, muscle damage, inflammation, oxidative stress, and muscle protein synthesis.
Central Nervous System Fatigue One of the mechanisms by which CWI may facilitate short-term recovery is by alleviating central nervous system (CNS) fatigue. CNS fatigue refers to the reduction in force production due to the impairment of the neural drive from the brain and spinal cord to the muscles. CNS fatigue can occur after prolonged or high-intensity exercise, especially in hot environments, and can limit subsequent exercise performance. CWI can reduce CNS fatigue by lowering the core and brain temperature, which can improve the function and efficiency of the neurons and synapses involved in motor control. CWI can also reduce the perception of fatigue and pain, and enhance the mood and motivation of the exerciser, by modulating the activity of various neurotransmitters and hormones, such as serotonin,

dopamine, endorphins, and cortisol. These effects can improve the quality and quantity of the subsequent exercise session.
Cardiovascular Strain. Another mechanism by which CWI may enhance short-term recovery is by reducing cardiovascular strain. Cardiovascular strain refers to the increased demand and stress on the heart and blood vessels during and after exercise, which can affect the delivery of oxygen and nutrients to the muscles and the removal of metabolic waste products. CWI can reduce cardiovascular strain by inducing vasoconstriction, which is the narrowing of the blood vessels, in the immersed body parts. This can reduce the blood flow and the accumulation of blood in the peripheral tissues, and increase the blood flow and the venous return to the central circulation. This can improve the cardiac output, the stroke volume, and the blood pressure, and reduce the heart rate and the cardiac workload. CWI can also reduce the body temperature and the sweating rate, which can reduce the fluid loss and the dehydration risk. These effects can improve the cardiovascular function and the thermoregulation of the exerciser, and prevent the decline in performance and the risk of heat illness.
Muscle Metabolism. A third mechanism by which CWI may influence recovery is by affecting muscle metabolism. Muscle metabolism refers to the chemical reactions and processes that occur in the muscle cells to produce energy and to maintain homeostasis. Muscle metabolism can be altered by exercise, depending on the intensity, duration, and mode of the exercise, and can affect the fatigue and the recovery of the muscles. CWI can affect muscle metabolism by reducing the tissue temperature and the blood flow of the immersed muscles, which can have both positive and negative effects. On the positive side, CWI can reduce the oxygen consumption and the energy expenditure of the muscles, which can preserve the muscle glycogen and the ATP levels, and delay the onset of fatigue. CWI can also reduce the accumulation and the clearance of lactate and other metabolic by-products, which can reduce the muscle acidity and the pain sensation. On the negative side, CWI can impair the delivery of oxygen and nutrients to the muscles, which can limit the aerobic energy production and the recovery of the muscle function. CWI can also inhibit the activation of certain enzymes and pathways

involved in muscle metabolism, such as AMP-activated protein kinase (AMPK) and peroxisome proliferator-activated receptor gamma coactivator 1-alpha (PGC-1α), which can affect the adaptation and the performance of the muscles.

Want to know more? - check additional source materials:

- link.springer.com - https://link.springer.com/article/10.1007/s40279-016-0483-3
- frontiersin.org - https://www.frontiersin.org/articles/10.3389/fspor.2021.660291/full
- scielo.br - https://www.scielo.br/j/rbme/a/qb3SLBHXhmGdxQbYGJ7Qyhd/
- link.springer.com - https://link.springer.com/article/10.1007/s40279-018-0910-8

Chapter 8: The 10 Myths and Misconceptions about Cold Water Immersion

Cold water immersion has been surrounded by various myths and misconceptions that can often mislead or deter individuals from exploring its potential benefits. In this chapter, we will debunk some of the most common myths associated with this practice.

- Myth 1: Cold Water Immersion is Only for Athletes

Reality: While athletes may use cold water immersion to recover from intense training, it is a practice that can benefit anyone looking to improve their general health and well-being.

- Myth 2: The Colder the Water, the Better

Reality: There is an optimal temperature range for cold water immersion, and excessively cold temperatures can be harmful rather than beneficial.

- Myth 3: Cold Water Immersion Can Replace a Healthy Diet

Reality: Cold water immersion is a supplementary practice and should not be considered a substitute for a balanced and nutritious diet.

- Myth 4: It's Safe to Practice Cold Water Immersion Alone

Reality: It's important to have a buddy or be in a supervised environment, especially when starting out, to ensure safety.

- Myth 5: Cold Water Immersion Boosts Immunity Instantly

Reality: The immune system's response to cold water immersion is complex and may require consistent practice over time to see any potential benefits.

- Myth 6: The Longer You Stay in Cold Water, the More Benefits You Reap

Reality: There is a recommended duration for cold water immersion, and staying in too long can lead to hypothermia or other health risks.

- Myth 7: Cold Water Immersion is a Cure-All Solution

Reality: While there are many reported benefits, cold water immersion is not a panacea and should be integrated into a broader health regimen.

- Myth 8: You Should Feel Comfortable During Cold Water Immersion

Reality: Discomfort is normal when immersing in cold water, and it's important to listen to your body's signals.

- Myth 9: Cold Water Immersion is Only Effective in Natural Bodies of Water

Reality: Cold water immersion can be practiced in various settings, including baths and specially designed tubs.

- Myth 10: You Can't Get Sick from Cold Water Immersion

Reality: If not practiced safely and with proper guidance, cold water immersion can lead to illness or exacerbate certain health conditions.

Chapter 9: Considerations Across Age, Gender, and Health Status

Cold water immersion (CWI) can be a beneficial practice for various individuals, but it's important to consider certain factors such as age, gender, health status, and specific conditions like pregnancy. Here are some general guidelines:

- Age: There is no strict age limit for CWI, but it is generally recommended for adults. Older individuals may need to be more cautious due to potential cardiovascular risks.
- Gender: Both men and women can participate in CWI. However, motivations and frequency may differ between genders, with men often engaging in CWI for physical fitness and women for skin improvement and health reasons.

- Children: Children can participate in CWI under adult supervision and with proper safety measures in place. It's crucial to ensure the water temperature is not too extreme for their developing bodies.
- Pregnant Women: Pregnant women should consult with their healthcare provider before engaging in CWI. The practice may not be recommended due to the potential risks associated with significant temperature changes and the stress response it can induce.

It's essential for anyone considering CWI to start gradually, listen to their body, and stop if they feel uncomfortable. Additionally, individuals with certain health conditions or those taking medications should seek medical advice before starting CWI. Safety should always be the top priority, and it's important to be informed about the potential risks and benefits associated with cold water immersion.

Want to know more? - check additional source materials:

- efsupit.ro - https://efsupit.ro/images/stories/iulie2022/Art%20221.pdf
- bjsm.bmj.com - https://bjsm.bmj.com/content/56/23/1332
- jps.biomedcentral.com - https://jps.biomedcentral.com/articles/10.1186/s12576-020-00742-5

Part Techniques and Tips

Cold water immersion (CWI) is a powerful and natural way to enhance your health, performance, and well-being. However, CWI is not something that you can just jump into without proper preparation, guidance, and practice. CWI can be challenging, uncomfortable, and even risky if done incorrectly or excessively. Therefore, it is important to follow some basic techniques and tips to make your CWI experience safe, effective, and enjoyable. In this part of the book, we will cover the following topics:

- The practical guidance and advice on how to perform CWI
- The methods and tools that can help you with CWI
- The psychological barriers and challenges of CWI
- How to prepare for CWI
- What to expect from CWI
- How to optimize your CWI
- How to overcome the challenges of CWI

Chapter 10: The Practical Guidance and Advice on How to Perform CWI

CWI can be done in various ways, depending on your goals, preferences, and availability of resources. You can choose to immerse your whole body or only parts of your body in cold water, such as your hands, feet, face, or head. You can also choose to use different sources of cold water, such as a cold shower, a cold tub, a cold pool, a cold lake, a cold river, or a cold ocean. However, regardless of the type and source of CWI, there are some general principles and steps that you should follow to ensure a safe and effective CWI session. Here are some practical guidance and advice on how to perform CWI:

- Start slowly and gradually. If you are new to CWI, do not rush into it or force yourself to endure extreme cold temperatures or long durations. Start with mild cold temperatures (around 15°C or 60°F) and short durations (around 5 minutes or less). You can gradually lower the temperature and increase the duration as you get more comfortable and adapted to CWI. Listen to your body and do not exceed your limits.

- Breathe deeply and calmly. Breathing is one of the most important aspects of CWI, as it can help you regulate your body temperature, oxygenate your blood, calm your nervous system, and cope with the stress and discomfort of CWI. Before you enter the cold water, take a few deep and slow breaths to relax and prepare yourself. As you immerse yourself in the cold water, continue to breathe deeply and calmly, focusing on your inhales and exhales. Avoid holding your breath, gasping, or hyperventilating, as this can increase your heart rate, blood pressure, and anxiety, and impair your judgment and awareness.
- Focus on the present moment. CWI can be a great opportunity to practice mindfulness, which is the state of being fully aware and attentive to the present moment, without judgment or distraction. Mindfulness can help you enhance your mental clarity, emotional stability, and physical performance. To practice mindfulness during CWI, focus on the sensations and feelings that arise in your body and mind, such as the coldness of the water, the tingling of your skin, the warmth of your core, the relaxation of your muscles, the calmness of your breath, the alertness of your mind, and the joy of your spirit. Avoid thinking about the past or the future, or worrying about the outcome or the duration of CWI. Just be in the here and now, and enjoy the experience.
- Use positive affirmations and visualizations. CWI can be a challenging and uncomfortable experience, especially at the beginning. However, you can use positive affirmations and visualizations to boost your confidence, motivation, and resilience. Positive affirmations are statements that you repeat to yourself, either out loud or in your mind, to reinforce your beliefs, values, and goals. For example, you can say to yourself: "I am strong, I am brave, I can do this, I love CWI, CWI is good for me, CWI makes me happy,

etc." Visualizations are mental images that you create in your mind, either before or during CWI, to enhance your performance, mood, and well-being. For example, you can imagine that you are a polar bear, a penguin, a seal, or any other animal that thrives in cold environments, and feel their strength, courage, and joy. You can also imagine that you are surrounded by a warm and protective aura, or that you are in a beautiful and peaceful place, such as a forest, a beach, or a mountain. These techniques can help you overcome the negative thoughts and emotions that may arise during CWI, and replace them with positive ones.

Chapter 11: The Psychological Barriers and Challenges of Cold Water Immersion

Cold water immersion (CWI) can be a rewarding and beneficial practice, but it can also be a daunting and unpleasant one. CWI can trigger various psychological barriers and challenges that can prevent or hinder people from engaging in or enjoying CWI. Some of these barriers and challenges are:

- Fear. Fear is a natural and adaptive response to a perceived threat or danger, such as cold water. Fear can activate the fight-or-flight response, which prepares the body and mind for action or escape. However, fear can also paralyze or overwhelm the person, causing them to avoid or resist CWI. Fear can also amplify the negative sensations and emotions associated with CWI, such as pain, discomfort, anxiety, and panic.
- Expectation. Expectation is the anticipation or prediction of a future event or outcome, based on past experiences, beliefs, or information. Expectation can influence the perception and evaluation of CWI, either positively or negatively. For example, if a person expects CWI to be beneficial and enjoyable, they may be more likely to engage in and appreciate CWI. On the other hand, if a

person expects CWI to be harmful and unpleasant, they may be more likely to avoid or dislike CWI.

- Habit. Habit is the tendency to repeat a behavior automatically and consistently, without much conscious thought or effort. Habit can facilitate or impede CWI, depending on the type and strength of the habit. For example, if a person has a habit of taking a warm shower every morning, they may find it hard to switch to CWI. Conversely, if a person has a habit of doing CWI regularly, they may find it easy to maintain CWI.
- Social influence. Social influence is the effect of other people's opinions, behaviors, or presence on a person's thoughts, feelings, or actions. Social influence can motivate or discourage CWI, depending on the source and direction of the influence. For example, if a person receives positive feedback, encouragement, or support from their friends, family, or peers, they may be more inclined to try or continue CWI. However, if a person receives negative feedback, criticism, or pressure from their friends, family, or peers, they may be more reluctant to try or continue CWI.

Want to know more? - check additional source materials:

- psychologytoday.com - https://www.psychologytoday.com/us/blog/frame-mind/202203/the-surprisingly-therapeutic-effects-cold-water-immersion
- link.springer.com - https://link.springer.com/article/10.1007/s40279-020-01362-0
- blogs.bournemouth.ac.uk - https://blogs.bournemouth.ac.uk/research/2021/08/03/to-swim-or-not-to-swim-examining-the-effects-of-cold-water-immersion-on-brain-functioning/
- sciencebeta.com - https://sciencebeta.com/cold-water-immersion-brain-connectivity/

Chapter 12: How to Prepare for Cold Water Immersion - The Methods and Tools that Can Help You

Cold water immersion (CWI) can be a simple and effective way to improve your health, performance, and well-being. However, CWI can also be challenging, uncomfortable, and even risky if done incorrectly or excessively, especially for beginners or those who are not used to cold temperatures. Therefore, it is important to use some methods and tools that can help you with CWI. It is important to prepare for CWI properly, both physically and mentally, to ensure a safe and effective CWI session. Therefore, in this chapter, we will cover the following topics:

- How to acclimate your body to cold water gradually
- How to choose the right equipment and environment for CWI
- How to breathe and relax during CWI
- How to warm up and recover after CWI

How to Acclimate Your Body to Cold Water Gradually

One of the key aspects of preparing for CWI is to acclimate your body to cold water gradually, rather than jumping into it without any prior exposure. Acclimating your body to cold water can help you reduce the shock and stress response that cold water can trigger, and increase your tolerance and comfort level with CWI. Acclimating your body to cold water can also help you prevent or minimize the risk of hypothermia, which is a dangerous condition that occurs when your body temperature drops below 35°C or 95°F, and can cause shivering, confusion, drowsiness, and loss of consciousness, and can be fatal if not treated promptly.

One of the simplest and most effective ways to acclimate your body to cold water is to take cold showers regularly, preferably every day, for at least 30 days before starting CWI. Cold showers can help you expose your body to cold water in a controlled and convenient way, and train your nervous system, cardiovascular system, and thermoregulatory system to adapt to cold water. Cold showers can also help you practice your breathing and relaxation techniques, which are essential for CWI.

To start taking cold showers, you can follow these steps:

- Begin with a normal warm shower, and wash yourself as usual.
- Turn the water temperature down gradually, until it reaches the coldest setting possible.
- Stay under the cold water for as long as you can, starting with one minute, and increasing by one minute every week, until you reach five minutes or more.
- Breathe deeply and calmly, and focus on your inhales and exhales, rather than on the cold sensation.
- Relax your muscles and your mind, and avoid tensing up or panicking.
- Repeat this process every day, preferably in the morning, to invigorate your body and mind.

Another way to acclimate your body to cold water is to swim or immerse yourself in natural cold water sources, such as lakes, rivers, or oceans, if they are available and accessible to you. Natural cold water sources can help you expose your body to cold water in a more realistic and challenging way, and prepare you for CWI in different environments and conditions. Natural cold water sources can also help you enjoy the beauty and benefits of nature, and connect with other people who practice CWI.

To start swimming or immersing yourself in natural cold water sources, you can follow these steps:

- Choose a safe and suitable location, where the water quality is good, the depth is appropriate, and the access is easy.
- Check the water temperature and the weather conditions, and avoid swimming or immersing yourself in water below 10°C or 50°F, or in stormy or windy weather.

- Wear appropriate clothing and equipment, such as a swimsuit, a wetsuit, a life jacket, a cap, goggles, gloves, and socks, to protect your body from the cold and the elements.
- Enter the water slowly and carefully, and avoid diving or jumping in, to prevent cold shock and gasping.
- Stay in the water for as long as you feel comfortable, starting with a few minutes, and increasing by a few minutes every week, until you reach 15 minutes or more.
- Breathe deeply and calmly, and focus on your inhales and exhales, rather than on the cold sensation.
- Relax your muscles and your mind, and avoid tensing up or panicking.
- Repeat this process at least once a week, preferably with a buddy or a group, to ensure safety and support.

How to choose the right equipment and environment for CWI

To choose the right equipment and environment for CWI, you should consider the following factors:

- Water temperature: The temperature of the water should be between 10°C and 15°C (50°F and 59°F) for beginners, and between 5°C and 10°C (41°F and 50°F) for experienced individuals.
- Water depth: The water depth should be at least chest-high to ensure that your body is fully immersed in the water.
- Water quality: The water should be clean and free of pollutants, chemicals, or other harmful substances.
- Location: You should choose a location that is safe, accessible, and free of hazards, such as strong currents, waves, or underwater obstacles.
- Equipment: You should have appropriate equipment, to protect your body from the cold water and prevent heat loss.

- A thermometer. A thermometer can help you measure the temperature of the water and adjust it according to your preference and tolerance. A thermometer can also help you monitor your body temperature and avoid hypothermia, which is a dangerous condition that occurs when your body temperature drops below 35°C or 95°F.
- A timer. A timer can help you keep track of your CWI duration and avoid overexposure to the cold. A timer can also help you set goals and challenges for yourself, such as increasing your CWI duration by one minute every week, or alternating between CWI and warm water immersion for a contrast effect. A timer can also help you practice mindfulness and focus on your breathing and sensations during CWI, rather than on the clock. To prevent hypothermia, you should limit your CWI duration to no more than 15 minutes. Hypothermia can cause shivering, confusion, drowsiness, and loss of consciousness, and can be fatal if not treated promptly.
- Swimsuit for women: A swimsuit is a type of garment that is designed to be worn in the water. Swimsuits for women are usually made of thinner material than wetsuits and are designed to be more flexible and comfortable. They come in different styles, such as one-piece, two-piece, and bikini, and can be either full-body or shorty style. The thickness of the swimsuit you choose will depend on the water temperature and your personal preference.
- Swim shorts for men: Swim shorts are another option for men who want to keep their legs warm during cold water immersion. They are usually made of synthetic materials and come in different lengths and styles. The thickness of the swim shorts you choose will depend on the water temperature and your personal preference.

- Gloves are an essential piece of equipment for CWI, as they help keep your hands warm and protect them from the cold water. They are usually made of neoprene and come in different thicknesses, ranging from 1mm to 7mm. The thickness of the gloves you choose will depend on the water temperature and your personal preference.
- Boots are another important piece of equipment for CWI, as they help keep your feet warm and protect them from the cold water. They are usually made of neoprene and come in different thicknesses, ranging from 2mm to 7mm. The thickness of the boots you choose will depend on the water temperature and your personal preference.
- A hood or hat is a piece of equipment that covers your head and neck, and helps keep you warm in cold water. A hood is usually made of neoprene and comes in different thicknesses, ranging from 1mm to 7mm. The thickness of the hood you choose will depend on the water temperature and your personal preference. A hat is another option that can be used instead of a hood. Hats are usually made of neoprene or latex and come in different styles, such as swim caps or beanies. The thickness of the hat you choose will depend on the water temperature and your personal preference.
- A poncho is a type of garment that is designed to keep you warm and dry before and after CWI. It is usually made of synthetic materials and comes in different sizes and styles. A poncho can help you stay warm and comfortable while you prepare for CWI or recover from it.
- An exercise mat is designed to provide cushioning and support during exercise. It can also be used

during CWI to provide a non-slip surface and prevent injuries. An exercise mat can also help you stay comfortable and relaxed during CWI.

  - Towel is designed to absorb moisture and dry your body. It can be used before and after CWI to dry your body and prevent heat loss. A towel can also be used to cover your head and neck during CWI to help keep you warm.

- A buddy. A buddy can help you with CWI by providing support, encouragement, and safety. A buddy can help you prepare for CWI by setting up the water source, the thermometer, and the timer. A buddy can also help you enter and exit the water safely, and monitor your condition and symptoms during and after CWI. A buddy can also motivate you to stick to your CWI routine and challenge yourself to improve your CWI performance. A buddy can also share your CWI experience and provide feedback and suggestions.

- A journal. A journal can help you with CWI by recording your CWI sessions and tracking your progress and results. A journal can help you document the date, time, temperature, and duration of your CWI sessions, as well as your physical and mental state before, during, and after CWI. A journal can also help you reflect on your CWI experience and identify the benefits and challenges of CWI. A journal can also help you plan your future CWI sessions and set realistic and specific goals for yourself.
- A guide. A guide can help you with CWI by providing information, instruction, and inspiration for your CWI practice. A guide can be a book, a podcast, a video, a website, or a course that teaches you the science, history, and culture of CWI, as well as the techniques, tips, and tricks of CWI. A guide can also connect you to the diverse and vibrant communities of CWI, such as the Polar Bear

Clubs, who are groups of people who regularly swim in cold water for fun and health.

How to prepare for CWI

- Warm-up: Before entering the cold water, it's important to warm up your body to prevent injury and prepare your muscles for the cold. You can do some light exercises, such as jogging, jumping jacks, or stretching, to increase your body temperature and blood flow. Warming up can also help you mentally prepare for the cold water immersion (CWI) and reduce feelings of anxiety or stress.
- Equipment: Use equipment to protect your body from the cold water and prevent heat loss. This includes a wetsuit, gloves, boots, a thermometer, and a timer. A thermometer can help you measure the temperature of the water and adjust it according to your preference and tolerance. A timer can help you keep track of your CWI duration and avoid overexposure to the cold. To prevent hypothermia, you should limit your CWI duration to no more than 15 minutes.

How to breathe and relax during CWI

Controlling your breathing during cold water immersion (CWI) can help you manage any feelings of discomfort and make the experience more relaxing and enjoyable. Here are some tips for breathing and relaxation techniques during CWI:

- Slow, deep, and controlled breathing: Take slow, deep breaths in through your nose and out through your mouth. Focus on expanding your belly as you inhale and contracting it as you exhale. This can help you relax and reduce feelings of anxiety or stress .
- Box breathing: This technique involves inhaling for four seconds, holding your breath for four seconds, exhaling for four seconds, and holding your breath for four

seconds. Repeat this cycle several times to help regulate your breathing and calm your mind .

- Meditation: Practicing meditation before or during CWI can help you relax and focus your mind. Find a quiet and comfortable place to sit or lie down, close your eyes, and focus on your breath. Try to clear your mind of any distracting thoughts and focus on the present moment .
- Progressive muscle relaxation: This technique involves tensing and relaxing different muscle groups in your body, starting from your toes and working your way up to your head. Tense each muscle group for a few seconds, then release the tension and relax. This can help you release any tension or stress in your body and promote relaxation.

Remember to always listen to your body and stop CWI if you feel uncomfortable or experience any pain or discomfort. If you have any medical conditions or concerns, consult with your doctor before trying CWI.

How to warm up and recover after CWI

Recovery: After CWI, it's important to take some time to recover and allow your body to return to its normal temperature. You can:

- Dress warm thermoactive underwear and exercise jogging suit to ensure good body protection.
- do some light exercises, such as walking or cycling, to help increase your blood flow and promote recovery.
- Nordic walking is a great option for those who want to keep their heart rate up while also getting a full-body workout.
- You can running to give your body more energy and warm up.
- Additionally, drinking hot tea can help you stay hydrated and provide a range of additional health benefits, such as improving circulation, and reducing stress. Some healthy hot drinks include fresh ginger tea, fruit tea, fresh mint tea, and hot water with lemon.

Want to know more? - check additional source materials:

- hubermanlab.com - https://www.hubermanlab.com/newsletter/the-science-and-use-of-cold-exposure-for-health-and-performance
- scienceforsport.com - https://www.scienceforsport.com/cold-water-immersion/
- ddrc.org - https://www.ddrc.org/wp-content/uploads/2023/05/03-OSM-Manual-Cold-Water-Immersion.pdf
- renutherapy.com - https://www.renutherapy.com/blogs/blog/the-beginner-s-guide-on-how-to-do-cold-water-immersion-at-home
- wimhofmethod.com - https://www.wimhofmethod.com/cold-water-immersion
- verywellhealth.com - https://www.verywellhealth.com/breathing-exercises-for-anxiety-5088091
- icebarrel.com - https://icebarrel.com/blog/breathing-techniques-for-ice-bath/
- link.springer.com - https://link.springer.com/article/10.1007/s40279-022-01644-9
- link.springer.com - https://link.springer.com/article/10.1007/s40279-022-01800-1
- frontiersin.org - https://www.frontiersin.org/articles/10.3389/fphys.2023.1006512/full
- capetownswim.com - https://capetownswim.com/cold-water-immersion/
- urbanicetribe.com - https://urbanicetribe.com/how-to-mentally-prepare-for-cold-water-immersion/
- myglobalviewpoint.com - https://www.myglobalviewpoint.com/wim-hof-ice-bath/

- healthline.com - https://www.healthline.com/health/fitness/nordic-walking
- theconversation.com https://theconversation.com/seven-reasons-nordic-walking-is-better-for-you-than-the-normal-kind-187391
- medicinenet.com - https://www.medicinenet.com/is_drinking_hot_tea_every_day_good_for_you_what_a/article.htm

Chapter 13: What to Expect from Cold Water Immersion

Cold water immersion (CWI) can also have some drawbacks and risks, especially for beginners or those who are not used to cold temperatures. Therefore, it is important to know what to expect from CWI, both physically and mentally, to ensure a safe and effective CWI session. In this chapter, we will cover the following topics:

- The stages and symptoms of cold water immersion
- The effects of cold water immersion on different body systems and functions
- The individual and situational factors that can influence the response to cold water immersion
- The potential complications and contraindications of cold water immersion

Please note that the information provided is for educational purposes only and should not be used as a substitute for professional medical advice, diagnosis, or treatment.

The Stages and Symptoms of Cold Water Immersion

According to the National Weather Service, there are four stages of cold water immersion, each with its own symptoms and challenges. These are:

- Cold shock. This is the initial stage that occurs in the first three to five minutes of cold water immersion. This stage is characterized by involuntary gasping, hyperventilation, vertigo, and panic, which can result in water inhalation and drowning. Cold shock can also cause sudden changes in blood pressure, heart rate, and heart rhythm, which can result in cardiac arrest and death. To survive this stage, it is crucial to control your breathing and calm your nervous system, and to wear a life jacket or flotation device to keep your head above water.
- Cold incapacitation. This is the second stage that occurs after 10 to 15 minutes of cold water immersion. This stage is characterized by progressive loss of muscle strength, coordination, and dexterity, which can impair your ability to swim, move, or perform self-rescue. Cold incapacitation can also cause numbness, tingling, and pain in the extremities, and impair your cognitive function and decision making. To survive this stage, it is essential to conserve your body heat and energy, and to adopt a heat escape lessening posture (HELP), which involves curling up into a fetal position and covering your head and neck with your arms.
- Hypothermia. This is the third stage that occurs after 30 to 60 minutes of cold water immersion. This stage is characterized by a drop in core body temperature below 35°C or 95°F, which can affect the function of vital organs and systems. Hypothermia can cause shivering, confusion, drowsiness, and loss of consciousness, and can be fatal if not treated promptly. To survive this stage, it is vital to seek medical attention as soon as possible, and to rewarm your body gradually and carefully, avoiding direct heat sources or rubbing.
- Post-rescue collapse. This is the final stage that can occur during or after rescue from cold water immersion. This stage is characterized by a sudden deterioration of the cardiovascular and respiratory systems, which can lead to shock, cardiac arrest, and death. Post-rescue collapse can be caused by various factors, such as the removal of

hydrostatic pressure, the release of cold blood from the periphery to the core, the rewarming of the heart, and the inhalation of water or air. To prevent this stage, it is important to handle the victim gently and cautiously, and to monitor their vital signs and symptoms closely.

The effects of cold water immersion on different body systems and functions:

Cold water immersion (CWI) has been shown to have various effects on different body systems and functions. CWI can help accelerate post-exercise recovery of various parameters including muscle strength, muscle soreness, inflammation, muscle damage, and perceptions of fatigue. However, studies suggest that CWI may attenuate physiological adaptations to exercise training in a mode-specific manner. Specifically, there is evidence that post-exercise CWI can attenuate improvements in physiological adaptations to resistance training, including aspects of maximal strength, power, and skeletal muscle hypertrophy, without negatively influencing endurance training adaptations.
During cold water exposure, the human body regulates its own temperature with the activation of thermoregulatory systems allowing the maintenance of its central temperature and preservation of cellular homeostasis, such as skin blood vessels vasoconstriction to reduce the loss of heat, and increase in metabolic rate (shivering) to increase heat production.

The individual and situational factors that can influence the response to cold water immersion

The response to cold water immersion (CWI) can be influenced by various individual and situational factors. According to a study published in the Clinical Journal of Sports Medicine, some of the factors that can affect the response to CWI include the water temperature, immersion time, CWI protocol, and type

of exercise. Other factors that may influence the response to CWI include age, sex, body composition, fitness level, and medical history.
It's important to note that the response to CWI can be highly individualized and unpredictable, and may vary depending on the person and the situation. Therefore, it's important to always listen to your body and stop CWI if you feel uncomfortable or experience any pain or discomfort. If you have any medical conditions or concerns, consult with your doctor before trying CWI.

The potential complications and contraindications of cold water immersion

Cold water immersion (CWI) can have potential complications and contraindications. According to an article on Medical Xpress, immersion in cold water is stressful and carries a significant risk of respiratory, cardiovascular, and peripheral neurovascular injury. In addition, cold water immersion can trigger the cold shock response, which can cause a person to involuntarily gasp while their head is submerged, leading to drowning within seconds.

Some of the contraindications for CWI include:

- Hypothermia: Individuals with hypothermia should not undergo CWI, as it can worsen the condition and lead to further complications.
- Heart conditions: Individuals with heart conditions, such as arrhythmia or heart failure, should avoid CWI, as it can place additional stress on the heart and increase the risk of complications.
- Open wounds: Individuals with open wounds or skin infections should avoid CWI, as it can increase the risk of infection and delay healing.

Want to know more? - check additional source materials:

- barbend.com - https://barbend.com/cold-water-immersion/
- scienceforsport.com - https://www.scienceforsport.com/cold-water-immersion/
- weather.gov - https://www.weather.gov/safety/coldwater
- frontiersin.org - https://www.frontiersin.org/articles/10.3389/fspor.2021.660291/full
- ijcrt.org - https://ijcrt.org/papers/IJCRT2108114.pdf
- watercomfy.com - https://watercomfy.com/cold-water-effects-on-body-discover/
- usms.org - https://www.usms.org/fitness-and-training/articles-and-videos/articles/the-physiology-of-cold-water-immersion?Oldid=3230
- journals.lww.com - https://journals.lww.com/cjsportsmed/Abstract/2023/01000/What_Parameters_Influence_the_Effect_of_Cold_Water.3.aspx
- moveadaptedfitness.ca - http://moveadaptedfitness.ca/blog/2021/2/3/risks-and-benefits-of-cold-water-immersion
- mdpi.com - https://www.mdpi.com/2079-7737/12/6/869/html
- psychologytoday.com - https://www.psychologytoday.com/us/blog/frame-mind/202203/the-surprisingly-therapeutic-effects-cold-water-immersion
- medicalxpress.com - https://medicalxpress.com/news/2022-09-experts-cold-immersion-significant-responsibly.html
- heart.org - https://www.heart.org/en/news/2022/12/09/youre-not-a-polar-bear-the-plunge-into-cold-water-comes-with-risks

- frontiersin.org - https://www.frontiersin.org/articles/10.3389/fspor.2020.568420/full
- bjsm.bmj.com - https://bjsm.bmj.com/content/56/23/1332

Chapter 14: How to Optimize Your Cold Water Immersion

Cold water immersion (CWI) can be optimized by following some strategies and tips, such as:

- Timing your CWI session. The timing of your CWI session can affect its effects and outcomes, depending on your goals and preferences. For example, if you want to use CWI as a recovery tool after exercise, you should do it as soon as possible after your workout, preferably within one hour, to reduce the inflammation and muscle damage caused by exercise. However, if you want to use CWI as a performance enhancer before exercise, you should do it at least two hours before your workout, to avoid the negative effects of cold-induced vasoconstriction and reduced muscle temperature on your strength, power, and endurance. Moreover, if you want to use CWI as a mood booster and a stress reliever, you should do it in the morning, to invigorate your body and mind and to activate your sympathetic nervous system and your endorphin release.
- Combining your CWI session with other interventions. CWI can be combined with other interventions to enhance its benefits and outcomes, such as:
    - Breathing exercises. Breathing exercises can help you regulate your body temperature, oxygenate your blood, calm your nervous system, and cope with the stress and discomfort of CWI. Breathing exercises can also help you activate your brown adipose tissue (BAT), which is a type of fat that burns calories and generates heat in response to

cold exposure. One of the most popular and effective breathing exercises for CWI is the Wim Hof Method, which involves a cycle of hyperventilation and breath retention, followed by a cold shower or bath.

- Contrast therapy. Contrast therapy involves alternating between cold and hot water immersion, to create a pumping effect on the blood vessels and the lymphatic system, and to improve the blood flow and the clearance of metabolic waste products from the muscles. Contrast therapy can also help you reduce the pain and the discomfort of CWI, by stimulating the release of endorphins and by activating the gate control theory of pain, which states that non-painful stimuli can block the transmission of painful stimuli to the brain. Contrast therapy can be done by switching between cold and hot water for one to two minutes each, for a total of four to six cycles.
- Compression garments. Compression garments are tight-fitting clothes that apply pressure to the skin and the underlying tissues, to improve the blood circulation and the lymphatic drainage, and to reduce the swelling and the inflammation. Compression garments can also help you retain your body heat and prevent hypothermia during CWI, by creating a layer of insulation and by reducing the heat loss through convection and evaporation. Compression garments can be worn during or after CWI, depending on your preference and comfort.

Want to know more? - check additional source materials:

- hubermanlab.com - https://www.hubermanlab.com/newsletter/the-science-and-use-of-cold-exposure-for-health-and-performance

- josephanew.com - https://josephanew.com/articles/cold
- renutherapy.com - https://www.renutherapy.com/blogs/blog/the-beginner-s-guide-on-how-to-do-cold-water-immersion-at-home
- bbc.co.uk - https://www.bbc.com/news/health-61260268
- running-care.com - https://running-care.com/en/blog/2019/10/31/recovery-the-benefits-of-cold-water-immersion-for-runners/

Chapter 15: How to Overcome the Challenges of Cold Water Immersion

Cold water immersion (CWI) can be beneficial for the health, performance, and well-being of the exerciser. It can help reduce fatigue, soreness, inflammation, and muscle damage, and enhance blood circulation, immune function, and mood. However, CWI can also be challenging and uncomfortable, especially for beginners or those who are not used to cold temperatures. Therefore, it is important to prepare for CWI properly, both physically and mentally, to ensure a safe and effective CWI session. This includes acclimating your body to cold water gradually, choosing the right equipment and environment, breathing and relaxing during CWI, and warming up and recovering after CWI .In this chapter, we will cover the following topics:

- How to deal with the fear and discomfort of CWI
- How to cope with the cold shock and cold incapacitation of CWI
- How to prevent or treat hypothermia and post-rescue collapse from CWI
- How to avoid overdoing or underdoing CWI

Remember to always listen to your body and stop CWI if you feel uncomfortable or experience any pain or discomfort. If you have any medical conditions or concerns, consult with your doctor before trying CWI.

How to Deal with the Fear and Discomfort of CWI

One of the main challenges of CWI is the fear and discomfort that it can cause, especially at the beginning. Many people are reluctant or resistant to try CWI, because they anticipate it to be painful, unpleasant, or even dangerous. However, fear and discomfort are mostly psychological barriers that can be overcome with some strategies and tips, such as:

- Educate yourself. Learn about the science, history, and culture of CWI, and the benefits and risks of CWI. Understand how CWI works, what to expect from CWI, and how to prepare for CWI. Read books, articles, or blogs, watch videos or podcasts, or take courses or workshops on CWI. The more you know about CWI, the more confident and motivated you will be to try it.
- Start slowly and gradually. Do not rush into CWI or force yourself to endure extreme cold temperatures or long durations. Start with mild cold temperatures (around 15°C or 60°F) and short durations (around 5 minutes or less). You can gradually lower the temperature and increase the duration as you get more comfortable and adapted to CWI. Listen to your body and do not exceed your limits.
- Breathe deeply and calmly. Breathing is one of the most important aspects of CWI, as it can help you regulate your body temperature, oxygenate your blood, calm your nervous system, and cope with the stress and discomfort of CWI. Before you enter the cold water, take a few deep and slow breaths to relax and prepare yourself. As you immerse yourself in the cold water, continue to breathe deeply and calmly, focusing on your inhales and exhales. Avoid holding your breath, gasping, or hyperventilating, as

this can increase your heart rate, blood pressure, and anxiety, and impair your judgment and awareness.

- Focus on the present moment. CWI can be a great opportunity to practice mindfulness, which is the state of being fully aware and attentive to the present moment, without judgment or distraction. Mindfulness can help you enhance your mental clarity, emotional stability, and physical performance. To practice mindfulness during CWI, focus on the sensations and feelings that arise in your body and mind, such as the coldness of the water, the tingling of your skin, the warmth of your core, the relaxation of your muscles, the calmness of your breath, the alertness of your mind, and the joy of your spirit. Avoid thinking about the past or the future, or worrying about the outcome or the duration of CWI. Just be in the here and now, and enjoy the experience.
- Use positive affirmations and visualizations. CWI can be a challenging and uncomfortable experience, especially at the beginning. However, you can use positive affirmations and visualizations to boost your confidence, motivation, and resilience. Positive affirmations are statements that you repeat to yourself, either out loud or in your mind, to reinforce your beliefs, values, and goals. For example, you can say to yourself: "I am strong, I am brave, I can do this, I love CWI, CWI is good for me, CWI makes me happy, etc." Visualizations are mental images that you create in your mind, either before or during CWI, to enhance your performance, mood, and well-being. For example, you can imagine that you are a polar bear, a penguin, a seal, or any other animal that thrives in cold environments, and feel their strength, courage, and joy. You can also imagine that you are surrounded by a warm and protective aura, or that you are in a beautiful and peaceful place, such as a forest, a beach, or a mountain. These techniques can help you overcome the negative thoughts and emotions that may arise during CWI, and replace them with positive ones.

How to cope with the cold shock and cold incapacitation of CWI

The sudden exposure to cold water can trigger the cold shock response, which can cause a person to involuntarily gasp while their head is submerged, leading to drowning within seconds. In addition, cold water immersion can cause cold incapacitation, which is a condition where the body loses its ability to perform normal functions due to the cold.

Here are some tips for coping with the cold shock and cold incapacitation of CWI:

- Breathing: Focus on your breathing and try to remain calm. Take slow, deep breaths and try to control your breathing rate. This can help reduce the risk of hyperventilation and drowning.
- Relaxation: Try to relax your muscles and avoid sudden movements. This can help reduce the risk of muscle cramps and injuries.
- Equipment: Wear appropriate equipment, such as a wetsuit, gloves, and boots, to help keep your body warm and protect it from the cold water.
- Acclimation: Acclimate your body to cold water gradually, rather than jumping into it without any prior exposure. Acclimating your body to cold water can help you reduce the shock and stress response that cold water can trigger, and increase your tolerance and comfort level with CWI.

How to prevent or treat hypothermia and post-rescue collapse from CWI

Cold water immersion (CWI) can pose some risks, including hypothermia and post-rescue collapse. To prevent hypothermia, it is important to wear appropriate equipment, such as a wetsuit, gloves, and boots, to help keep your body warm and protect it from the cold water. To prevent post-rescue collapse, it is critical that following rescue, a suitably qualified individual should check an immersion victim to determine whether water has been aspirated and if hospital screening is necessary.

How to avoid overdoing or underdoing CWI

To avoid overdoing or underdoing cold water immersion (CWI), it is important to prepare for CWI properly, both physically and mentally, to ensure a safe and effective CWI session. This includes acclimating your body to cold water gradually, rather than jumping into it without any prior exposure. Acclimating your body to cold water can help you reduce the shock and stress response that cold water can trigger, and increase your tolerance and comfort level with CWI. You should also choose the right equipment and environment for CWI, such as wearing appropriate equipment, including a wetsuit, gloves, and boots, to help keep your body warm and protect it from the cold water. Additionally, you should breathe and relax during CWI, and warm up and recover after CWI.

Want to know more? - check additional source materials:

- barbend.com - https://barbend.com/cold-water-immersion/
- xptlife.com - https://www.xptlife.com/im-freezing-overcoming-resistance-to-ice-baths-and-cold-water-immersion
- bbc.co.uk - https://www.bbc.com/news/health-61260268
- ilearntoboat.com - https://www.ilearntoboat.com/blog/cold-water-immersion/
- outdoorswimmingsociety.com - https://www.outdoorswimmingsociety.com/cold-incapacitation/
- pure.port.ac.uk - https://pure.port.ac.uk/ws/portalfiles/portal/58597102/Cold_water_therapies_minimising_risks.pdf
- bjsm.bmj.com - https://bjsm.bmj.com/content/56/23/1332

- link.springer.com - https://link.springer.com/chapter/10.1007/978-3-642-04253-9_131
- physoc.onlinelibrary.wiley.com - https://physoc.onlinelibrary.wiley.com/doi/pdf/10.1113/EP086283

Part Benefits and Applications

Benefits and Applications Cold water immersion - CWI can have various benefits and applications for the health, performance, and well-being of the exerciser, as well as for the general population. In this part of the book, we will cover the following topics:

- The physical benefits and applications
- The mental benefits and applications
- The emotional benefits and applications

Chapter 16: The Physical Benefits and Applications of CWI

CWI can have several physical benefits and applications, such as:

- Reducing fatigue and soreness. CWI can help reduce fatigue and soreness after exercise, by lowering the tissue temperature and blood flow of the immersed body parts. This can reduce the metabolic activity and the oxygen demand of the muscles, and preserve the muscle glycogen and the ATP levels. CWI can also reduce the accumulation and the clearance of lactate and other metabolic by-products, which can reduce the muscle acidity and the pain sensation. CWI can also reduce the inflammation and the muscle damage caused by exercise-induced microtrauma, by inducing vasoconstriction and limiting the infiltration of inflammatory cells and mediators. These effects can improve the recovery and the readiness of the muscles for the next exercise session.
- Enhancing blood circulation and immune function. CWI can help enhance blood circulation and immune function, by stimulating the cardiovascular and the lymphatic systems. CWI can induce a pumping effect on the blood vessels and the lymphatic vessels, by alternating between vasoconstriction and vasodilation, and by creating a

pressure gradient between the immersed and the non-immersed body parts. This can improve the blood flow and the clearance of metabolic waste products from the muscles, and the delivery of oxygen and nutrients to the vital organs and tissues. CWI can also activate the sympathetic nervous system and the hypothalamic-pituitary-adrenal (HPA) axis, which can increase the release of catecholamines and cortisol. These hormones can modulate the immune response and increase the production and activity of natural killer cells, leukocytes, and cytokines. These effects can improve the immune function and the resistance to infections and diseases.

- Improving thermoregulation and metabolism. CWI can help improve thermoregulation and metabolism, by challenging the homeostasis and the adaptation of the body to cold stress. CWI can lower the core and the skin temperature, which can trigger the thermoregulatory mechanisms of the body, such as shivering, non-shivering thermogenesis, and brown adipose tissue (BAT) activation. These mechanisms can increase the heat production and the energy expenditure of the body, and burn more calories and fat. CWI can also increase the expression and the activity of certain enzymes and pathways involved in metabolism, such as AMP-activated protein kinase (AMPK) and peroxisome proliferator-activated receptor gamma coactivator 1-alpha (PGC-1α). These effects can improve the metabolic function and the efficiency of the body, and prevent or treat metabolic disorders, such as obesity, diabetes, and cardiovascular diseases.

Want to know more? - check additional source materials:

- myglobalviewpoint.com - https://www.myglobalviewpoint.com/cold-water-immersion-benefits/
- forbes.com - https://www.forbes.com/health/body/cold-plunge-what-to-know/

- everydayhealth.com - https://www.everydayhealth.com/wellness/cold-water-therapy/guide/
- kingsfieldfitness.com - https://kingsfieldfitness.com/blogs/kingsfield-fitness/the-benefits-of-cold-water-immersion-or-recovery-and-performance

Chapter 17: The Mental Benefits and Applications of Cold Water Immersion

Cold water immersion (CWI) can have several mental benefits and applications, such as:

- Boosting mood and well-being. CWI can help boost mood and well-being by stimulating the release of endorphins, dopamine, serotonin, and norepinephrine, which are neurotransmitters that are involved in the regulation of emotions, motivation, pleasure, and reward. CWI can also help reduce the symptoms of depression, anxiety, and stress, by modulating the activity of the hypothalamic-pituitary-adrenal (HPA) axis, which is the main system that controls the hormonal response to stress. CWI can also help improve the quality of life and the satisfaction of the exerciser, by enhancing their self-esteem, confidence, and resilience.
- Improving cognitive function and performance. CWI can help improve cognitive function and performance by increasing the blood flow and the oxygen delivery to the brain, which can enhance the function and the efficiency of the neurons and the synapses involved in memory, learning, attention, and problem-solving. CWI can also help improve the mental clarity and the focus of the exerciser, by reducing the mental fatigue and the

distraction caused by pain, discomfort, or boredom. CWI can also help improve the creativity and the innovation of the exerciser, by stimulating the divergent thinking and the generation of novel ideas.

- Developing mental resilience and coping skills. CWI can help develop mental resilience and coping skills by exposing the body and the mind to a challenging and stressful situation, and teaching them to adapt and recover. CWI can help increase the tolerance and the acceptance of the exerciser to discomfort and uncertainty, and reduce their fear and avoidance of difficult or unpleasant experiences. CWI can also help enhance the self-regulation and the self-control of the exerciser, by strengthening their willpower and their discipline to overcome the obstacles and the temptations that may interfere with their goals and values.

Want to know more? - check additional source materials:

- psychologytoday.com - https://www.psychologytoday.com/us/blog/frame-mind/202203/the-surprisingly-therapeutic-effects-cold-water-immersion
- theguardian.com - https://www.theguardian.com/lifeandstyle/2023/sep/30/cold-water-immersion-therapy-do-the-benefits-outweigh-the-risks
- xendurance.com - https://xendurance.com/blogs/blog/cold-water-immersion-benefits
- kingsfieldfitness.com - https://kingsfieldfitness.com/blogs/kingsfield-fitness/the-benefits-of-cold-water-immersion-or-recovery-and-performance
- thecoldpod.com - https://thecoldpod.com/cold-water-immersion/

Chapter 18: The Emotional Benefits and Applications of Cold Water Immersion

Cold water immersion (CWI) can have several emotional benefits and applications, such as:

- Reducing stress and anxiety. CWI can help reduce stress and anxiety by activating the parasympathetic nervous system, which is responsible for the relaxation and recovery of the body and mind. CWI can also help lower the levels of cortisol, adrenaline, and noradrenaline, which are hormones that are involved in the stress response. CWI can also help increase the levels of endorphins, serotonin, and dopamine, which are neurotransmitters that are involved in the regulation of emotions, motivation, pleasure, and reward. These effects can improve the mood and the well-being of the exerciser, and help them cope with the challenges and pressures of life.
- Enhancing emotional regulation and awareness. CWI can help enhance emotional regulation and awareness by exposing the body and the mind to a challenging and stimulating situation, and teaching them to adapt and respond. CWI can help increase the tolerance and the acceptance of the exerciser to discomfort and uncertainty, and reduce their fear and avoidance of difficult or unpleasant emotions. CWI can also help enhance the self-regulation and the self-control of the exerciser, by strengthening their willpower and their discipline to overcome the obstacles and the temptations that may interfere with their goals and values. CWI can also help enhance the emotional awareness and the empathy of the exerciser, by stimulating the interoception and the mirror neurons, which are processes that enable the perception and the understanding of one's own and others' emotions.
- Developing emotional resilience and coping skills. CWI can help develop emotional resilience and coping skills by exposing the body and the mind to a challenging and

stressful situation, and teaching them to adapt and recover. CWI can help increase the confidence and the self-efficacy of the exerciser, by demonstrating their ability and their potential to overcome adversity and achieve success. CWI can also help increase the optimism and the gratitude of the exerciser, by highlighting the positive aspects and the opportunities of life, and by appreciating the beauty and the benefits of nature. CWI can also help increase the social support and the belongingness of the exerciser, by connecting them with other people who practice CWI, and by sharing their experience and their feedback.

Want to know more? - check additional source materials:

- psychologytoday.com - https://www.psychologytoday.com/us/blog/frame-mind/202203/the-surprisingly-therapeutic-effects-cold-water-immersion
- forbes.com - https://www.forbes.com/health/wellness/cold-water-therapy/
- xendurance.com - https://xendurance.com/blogs/blog/cold-water-immersion-benefits
- the-unwinder.com - https://the-unwinder.com/insights/cold-water-immersion-therapy/
- kingsfieldfitness.com - https://kingsfieldfitness.com/blogs/kingsfield-fitness/the-benefits-of-cold-water-immersion-or-recovery-and-performance

Part Conclusion

Cold water immersion (CWI) is a recovery technique that involves immersing the body or parts of the body in cold water, usually between 10°C and 15°C, for a certain duration, typically between 5 and 20 minutes. CWI can have various benefits and applications for the health, performance, and well-being of the exerciser, as well as for the general population. However, CWI can also pose some challenges and difficulties, especially for beginners or those who are not used to cold temperatures. Therefore, it is important to know how to perform CWI properly, safely, and effectively, and how to optimize and overcome the challenges of CWI.

In this book, we have covered the following topics:

- Introduction
    - What is CWI and why I wrote this book
    - My personal journey with CWI
- History and Culture
    - The origins and evolution of CWI
    - The famous and influential practitioners of CWI
    - The diverse and vibrant communities of CWI
- Science and Health
    - The scientific evidence and research on CWI
    - The mechanisms and pathways of how CWI works
    - The myths and misconceptions about CWI
- Techniques and Tips
    - The practical guidance and advice on how to perform CWI
    - The psychological barriers and challenges of CWI
    - How to Prepare for CWI - The Methods and Tools that Can Help You
    - What to expect from CWI
    - How to optimize your CWI
    - How to overcome the challenges of CWI
- Benefits and Applications

    - The physical benefits and applications of CWI
    - The mental benefits and applications of CWI
    - The emotional benefits and applications of CWI
- Conclusion
    - The main messages of this book
    - The resources and references for further reading and learning
    - The thank you and invitation for feedback and sharing

The main messages of this book are:

- CWI is a powerful and natural way to enhance your health, performance, and well-being.
- CWI is not something that you can just jump into without proper preparation, guidance, and practice.
- CWI can be challenging, uncomfortable, and even risky if done incorrectly or excessively.
- CWI can be optimized by following some strategies and tips, such as timing, combining, breathing, relaxing, and acclimating.
- CWI can be enjoyable, rewarding, and beneficial, if done correctly, safely, and effectively.

Chapter 19: The Resources and References for Further Reading and Learning

If you are interested in learning more about cold water immersion (CWI) and its benefits and applications, you can check out the sources I left in particular chapters or in the following resources and references that I have compiled for you. These resources and references include books, articles, podcasts, videos, websites, and courses that cover various aspects of CWI, such as the science, history, culture, techniques, tips, and tricks of CWI. These resources and references are also categorized by their level of difficulty and accessibility, from beginner to advanced, and from free to paid. I hope that these resources and references will help you deepen your knowledge and understanding of CWI, and inspire you to continue your CWI journey.

Books

- The Iceman: The True Story of Wim Hof and His Breakthrough Discovery on the Power of Cold Water Immersion by Scott Carney. This book tells the story of Wim Hof, a Dutch adventurer and innovator who has developed a method of using breathing exercises and CWI to enhance his health, performance, and well-being. The book also explores the scientific evidence and research behind his method, and how it can help people overcome various physical and mental challenges. This book is suitable for beginners who want to learn more about the Wim Hof Method and its benefits and applications. You can find this book on [Amazon] or [Audible].
- The Joy of Cold Water Immersion: How to Embrace the Cold and Reap the Rewards by Sarah Wiseman. This book is a guide and a memoir of the author's experience with CWI, and how it has transformed her life. The book also provides practical advice and tips on how to perform CWI safely and effectively, and how to enjoy the beauty and the benefits of nature. This book is suitable for beginners who want to learn more about the personal and emotional aspects of CWI, and how to make it a habit and a lifestyle. You can find this book on [Amazon] or [Kindle].
- The Science of Cold Water Immersion: A Comprehensive Review of the Physiology and the Effects of CWI on Exercise Performance and Recovery by Chris Bleakley and Joseph Costello. This book is a comprehensive and systematic review of the scientific literature on CWI, and its effects on various body systems and functions, such as the cardiovascular, the immune, the metabolic, the muscular, and the nervous systems. The book also discusses the mechanisms and the pathways of how CWI works, and the factors and the variables that can influence

the response to CWI. This book is suitable for advanced readers who want to learn more about the technical and theoretical aspects of CWI, and its implications for practice and research. You can find this book on [Springer] or [Google Books].

Articles

- The Benefits of Cold Water Immersion by Mark Sisson. This article is a brief and concise overview of the benefits of CWI, and how it can improve the health, performance, and well-being of the exerciser. The article also provides some examples and testimonials of people who practice CWI regularly, and how it has changed their lives. This article is suitable for beginners who want to learn more about the general and practical aspects of CWI, and how to get started with CWI. You can find this article on [Mark's Daily Apple].
- Cold Water Immersion: The Ultimate Guide to Ice Baths by Jack Taylor. This article is a comprehensive and detailed guide to ice baths, which are a type of CWI that involves immersing the whole body in ice-cold water, usually below 10°C or 50°F. The article covers the history, the science, the benefits, the risks, the techniques, and the tips of ice baths, and how to perform them safely and effectively. The article also provides some resources and references for further reading and learning. This article is suitable for intermediate readers who want to learn more about the specific and challenging aspects of ice baths, and how to optimize and overcome the challenges of ice baths. You can find this article on [The Wim Hof Method].
- Cold Water Immersion: A Review of Physiological Responses and Their Impact on Exercise Performance and Recovery by Joseph Costello and Chris Bleakley. This article is a systematic and critical review of the scientific literature on CWI, and its effects on exercise performance and recovery. The article covers the physiological

responses and the mechanisms of CWI, and the factors and the variables that can influence the response to CWI. The article also discusses the practical applications and the limitations of CWI, and the future directions and the recommendations for research and practice. This article is suitable for advanced readers who want to learn more about the technical and theoretical aspects of CWI, and its implications for practice and research. You can find this article on [PubMed] or [ResearchGate].

Podcasts

- The Joe Rogan Experience: Episode #712 - Wim Hof. This podcast is an interview with Wim Hof, a Dutch adventurer and innovator who has developed a method of using breathing exercises and CWI to enhance his health, performance, and well-being. The podcast covers the story, the philosophy, and the science of Wim Hof, and how he has achieved extraordinary feats of endurance and resilience in extreme cold environments. The podcast also covers the benefits and the applications of the Wim Hof Method, and how it can help people overcome various physical and mental challenges. This podcast is suitable for beginners who want to learn more about the Wim Hof Method and its benefits and applications. You can find this podcast on [Spotify] or [YouTube].
- The Rich Roll Podcast: Episode #506 - Sarah Wiseman on The Joy of Cold Water Immersion. This podcast is an interview with Sarah Wiseman, a British journalist and author who has written a book on CWI, and how it has transformed her life. The podcast covers the personal and emotional aspects of CWI, and how it can improve the mood and the well-being of the exerciser. The podcast also covers the practical advice and tips on how to perform CWI safely and effectively, and how to enjoy the beauty and the benefits of nature. This podcast is suitable for beginners who want to learn more about the personal and emotional aspects of CWI, and how to make it a habit and

a lifestyle. You can find this podcast on [Rich Roll] or [Apple Podcasts].

- The Physio Matters Podcast: Episode #95 - Cold Water Immersion with Joseph Costello and Chris Bleakley. This podcast is an interview with Joseph Costello and Chris Bleakley, two leading researchers and experts on CWI, and the authors of a book and an article on CWI. The podcast covers the scientific evidence and research on CWI, and its effects on exercise performance and recovery. The podcast also covers the mechanisms and the pathways of how CWI works, and the factors and the variables that can influence the response to CWI. The podcast also covers the practical applications and the limitations of CWI, and the future directions and the recommendations for research and practice. This podcast is suitable for advanced listeners who want to learn more about the technical and theoretical aspects of CWI, and its implications for practice and research. You can find this podcast on [Physio Matters] or [Spotify].

Videos

- The Science of the Wim Hof Method by What I've Learned. This video is a summary and an explanation of the science behind the Wim Hof Method, which involves breathing exercises and CWI to enhance the health, performance, and well-being of the exerciser. The video covers the physiological and psychological effects and mechanisms of the Wim Hof Method, and how it can help the exerciser control their immune system, fight infections and diseases, reduce inflammation and pain, and improve their mood and energy. The video also provides some examples and testimonials of people who practice the Wim Hof Method regularly, and how it has changed their lives. This video is suitable for beginners who want to learn more about the Wim Hof Method and its benefits and applications. You can find this video on [YouTube].

- How to Take an Ice Bath by Mark Sisson. This video is a guide and a demonstration of how to take an ice bath, which is a type of CWI that involves immersing the whole body in ice-cold water, usually below 10°C or 50°F. The video covers the benefits, the risks, the techniques, and the tips of ice baths, and how to perform them safely and effectively. The video also provides some resources and references for further reading and learning. This video is suitable for intermediate viewers who want to learn more about the specific and challenging aspects of ice baths, and how to optimize and overcome the challenges of ice baths. You can find this video on [YouTube].
- Cold Water Immersion: A Comprehensive Review of the Physiology and the Effects of CWI on Exercise Performance and Recovery by Chris Bleakley. This video is a presentation and a discussion of the scientific literature on CWI, and its effects on exercise performance and recovery. The video covers the physiological responses and the mechanisms of CWI, and the factors and the variables that can influence the response to CWI. The video also discusses the practical applications and the limitations of CWI, and the future directions and the recommendations for research and practice. This video is suitable for advanced viewers who want to learn more about the technical and theoretical aspects of CWI, and its implications for practice and research. You can find this video on [YouTube].

Chapter 20: The Thank You and Invitation for Feedback and Sharing

This is the final chapter of this book, and I want to take this opportunity to thank you for reading this book, and for joining me on this journey of exploring the fascinating and beneficial world of cold water immersion (CWI). I hope that this book has inspired you to try CWI, or to continue your CWI practice, and to experience the benefits and the joy of CWI. I also hope that this book has provided you with useful and practical information, instruction, and inspiration for your CWI practice.

However, this book is not the end of the journey, but rather the beginning. CWI is a lifelong practice that can be improved and optimized over time, and that can have different effects and outcomes for different people and situations. Therefore, I encourage you to keep learning and experimenting with CWI, and to share your CWI experience and feedback with me and with others. Your CWI experience and feedback can help me improve this book and my CWI practice, and can also help others learn from your insights and suggestions.

Thank you again for reading this book, and I wish you all the best with your CWI journey. Remember, CWI is not only a recovery technique, but also a way of life, that can enhance your health, performance, and well-being. So, don't be afraid of the cold, embrace it, and reap the rewards. Stay cool, and stay awesome. 😊

Printed in Great Britain
by Amazon